Un-Settling

The Modern Woman's Guide to
Getting What You Really Want
Out of Work and Life

Un-Settling

The Modern Woman's Guide to Getting What You Really Want Out of Work and Life

By Lys Ella Severtson

www.YouSpeakItPublishing.com

Copyright © 2016 Lys Ella Severtson

All rights reserved. No part of this book may be reproduced or transmitted in any form or by any means without written permission of the publisher, except in the case of brief quotations embodied in critical articles and reviews.

This material has been written and published solely for educational purposes. The author and the publisher shall have neither liability nor responsibility to any person or entity with respect to any loss, damage, or injury caused or alleged to be caused directly or indirectly by the information contained in this book.

Statements made and opinions expressed in this publication are those of the author and do not necessarily reflect the views of the publisher or indicate an endorsement by the publisher.

ISBN: 978-1-945446-14-6

Dedication

To my family, both nuclear and extended, for allowing me this expression of my work. May I live to see the day when every woman in this world believes that her options are unlimited regardless of her gender.

Acknowledgments

Abby, Alan, Ann, Artemis, Clare, Coco, Jenna, Lisa, Lisa Maria, Liz, Lynda, Nina, Peter, Steve: you trusted me to take you on your own un-settling journeys. In turn, you increased the pride and joy I feel for having known you and worked with you. I'm forever grateful.

Melissa Ford, Teacher, Questioner, Nonbeliever of Fearful Reasoning: thank you.

Cristina and Lenelle: You helped me through life transitions with wise insight, shared meals, and childcare. Never forgotten.

Todd: You make me better.

Contents

Introduction	11

CHAPTER 1
What Do You Want?	17
Be Specific	17
Include Everything You *Really* Want, Not Just What You Think You *Should* Want	22
This Is You Authoring Your Future	26

CHAPTER 2
Why Do You Want It?	35
How Do You Feel About It?	35
What Would Un-Settling Do?	38
Is There Any Part Of Your *Why* That Makes You Uncomfortable?	42

CHAPTER 3
What's Stopping You?	49
Make A List	49
They're All Excuses	52
Did I Mention That They're All Excuses?	56

CHAPTER 4
    Are You Ashamed or Scared? —
      The Crying Chapter   65
        What Haven't You Written Down Yet That You Know Is Still Casting A Shadow Over This Process?   65
        You're Not Alone   70
        Do You Want To Believe A New Story?   76

CHAPTER 5
    What Are You Willing to Do About It?   83
      Actions Are All That Matter   83
      The Psychology Of Setting Micro-Goals   86
      Focus On One, Not Many   90

Conclusion   97

Next Steps   99

About the Author   101

Introduction

This book is about taking actions in order to create a future for yourself that you have long envisioned, but have not yet acted upon. It's a how-to manual that leads you to action-steps. It specifically covers everything that has to be in place in order for you take action. The book examines all the mental stuff getting in your way that you may or may not be aware of so that you can see it, sort it out, and prepare yourself to step forward.

I wrote this book for two reasons. The first reason is I have personally found so much joy in un-settling myself and creating a future for myself. My only regret is that fear kept me stuck for seven years before I took the steps to create this life I love. My mission is to encourage other women to act now — not to wait as I did. You don't have to settle. If by reading this book, even one woman finds the courage to un-settle and act now to create the life she loves, I will feel that my mission has been accomplished.

The second reason for the creation of this book is it is un-settling to meet so many women who feel like they can't make changes in their life. They've settled, and the settling has turned into resentment, a feeling of powerlessness, and physical and mental distress. Women don't need to settle anymore. This book provides a process and a plan to show you how to *stop settling for less than you want* in your life starting right now. It is a vehicle to reach the masses of women who need a catalyst for change but whom I could never meet in person.

I want to distinguish the difference between being *unsettled*—not calm or tranquil, not decided, not determined—with *un-settled*, meaning specifically *not* compromising the self. So the word is hyphenated throughout this book.

Read the book in order. It's specifically organized to take you through the process of un-settling step by step. You may find some of the exercises to be challenging, and you may be tempted to skip over them if you feel uncomfortable. Do your best to complete them. If you get stuck, it may be best for you to move on and then come back to the exercises you skipped at a later time.

I hope you will gain clarity about exactly what you want for yourself. Clarity creates choice. With clarity, you will either decide you are willing to go after your dream and commit to take action in order to make it happen, or you will decide that your dream is not something you're willing to pursue at the moment. The beauty of either option is that it moves you out of a space of ambiguity. Getting clear is the first step toward a happier life.

Becoming un-settled puts you in the driver's seat, free to choose what is right for you in the moment. Enjoy the journey.

Chapter *1*

What Do You Want?

BE SPECIFIC

Having vague ideas about what you want makes it difficult to put a plan into action. As you work through the process of un-settling, paint a vivid picture of the life you want to create with specific details that will help you bring it to life. You can find downloadable worksheets on my website at www.lysella.com.

Specificity Focuses Your Mind and Your Actions

My story is a perfect example of the power of specificity. I was unhappy in my corporate career and my marriage, and thought about making changes in my life for about seven years before I took the first steps. Most of those years were spent in a vague dream state where I would drift in and out of discontent.

While I thought there was something else better for me, I would only dream about it occasionally and attempt to identify what that better thing might be. However, I never articulated what I wanted specifically. I struggled because my marriage didn't look like what I thought a marriage was supposed to look like, and I began to pay attention to how different my husband and I were: I loved social events; my husband did not. My husband didn't commit to doing stuff and even refused to help around the house.

I realized how important it is for me to be in a marriage that is an equal partnership.

Finally, my dissatisfaction with the situation motivated me to get specific. I wrote down exactly what I wanted my new life to contain. That specificity allowed me to look at my dream on paper and then decide if that was exactly what I wanted. Once I could see what it was, I could add to and subtract from it until I had incorporated all of the aspects of my life in their most perfect form. I was able to get excited and start taking actions toward making my dream life a reality. Without specificity, my thoughts would have remained dreams.

Include All Aspects of Your Life

Often when I ask someone what their dream life would look like, whether their topic is a career change or something else they want in their life, their response is usually broad and limiting like:

- *Oh, well, I'd be in a career that's more creative.*
- *I'd make more money.*
- *I wouldn't be as stressed out as I am now.*

That's a good start, but you can and need to go so much deeper.

When my coach, Melissa Ford, challenged me to go deeper, I hesitated. With Melissa's encouragement, my true desires eventually came out. I had specific ideas about what I wanted in a career and lifestyle. It was also important to me to no longer blame my husband any time I felt bad and to decide if I could be okay with our version of marriage, even if it was not exactly what I had always thought a good marriage should be.

Challenge yourself to examine every single aspect of your life and to write down how your perfect life would look.

- What do your weekdays look like?
- What do the weekends look like?
- What are the activities that fill your days?
- How many hours a day are you spending doing different kinds of activities?
- Are you satisfied with the compensation you receive for your services?
- Where do you live?

- What do you like about your community?
- With whom do you interact?
- With whom do you prefer *not* to interact?
- When do you do things you don't want to do out of obligation: often, sometimes, or never?
- When do you act alone?
- When do you involve a partner?
- Do you travel?
- What do you eat?
- How do you take care of your body?
- Which parts of your life feel like you've settled?
- In which areas of your life do you want to shake things up?

Ask yourself these questions and include your responses to them in the life plan you're designing for yourself. This is the foundation for creating the life of your dreams and never settling again.

Editing What You Want

This section is about removing any perfectionist tendencies you might have as you go through the exercises and worksheets. Editing serves a purpose. The first things that come into your mind are often great ideas and are often the correct indicators of where you want to go or what you want to do. In terms of designing a plan for your future, editing is completely permissible, and an important part of the process.

People have a tendency to believe that once they write down what they want, it's permanent—set in stone. That's absolutely false. Your plan is a living, breathing, fluid representation of what you want next. As you make more decisions and discover more about yourself, your world, and the things that excite you, it's perfectly natural to edit your list. By revisiting and editing your plan, you're continually recalibrating yourself. You're continually adjusting your path toward your new, most complete future.

There is a magic that happens when you look back at something that you wrote down as your goal or what you thought your future was going to look like after a few months. It is fascinating to see how both how your goal has morphed and changed over time and to see how much you've accomplished. If you haven't already completed the worksheets, I encourage you to do that now. You can find downloadable worksheets on my website at www.lysella.com. Even if you don't go any further, completing the worksheets now will give you a reference to look back on a month from now, three months from now, or a year from now.

INCLUDE EVERYTHING YOU *REALLY* WANT, NOT JUST WHAT YOU THINK YOU *SHOULD* WANT

This section digs deeper into the concept of editing your desired future. If you haven't already gotten the theme of the book, this is where you are asked to really un-settle yourself. Question whether what you have written down on your worksheet is influenced slightly or heavily by what you have been told at some point in your life is what you *should* want. You will be challenged to decide what you truly want, regardless of what those who are closest to you might think you should want.

What Have You Been Told You Can't Have?

Here is the life story of an amazing woman, Cosette Leary, who graciously gave me permission to share it with you.

Cosette was told from a young age that she could never escape poverty. She was born into poverty, grew up in poverty, and raised her four children as a single mother in poverty. Every social cue from her family, friends, and connections told her that this was her life, and that she needed to learn to live with it.

But Cosette didn't believe what everyone else believed. She clung to the hope instilled in her by her late father and mentor. He kept the spark within her alive, fueled by their belief that she could have a better life, no matter what other people told her.

Cosette set out a plan for herself to accomplish what she wanted. She wanted to go to college, work on Capitol Hill, earn more than minimum wage, and ultimately, identify what she had to share with the world and share it on a stage. She slowly began to check these things off her list over the course of thirteen years.

She is now a speaker on the topic of poverty elimination. She educates social workers on approaches that create real change when working with people in poverty. She also advocates changes to government policy to speed up the elimination of poverty. Finally, she works with individuals who have lived in poverty to instill a sense of hope that an escape from poverty is possible.

This is a dramatic story about not letting what you've been told you can't have stop you from designing a life you love. Let this serve as an inspiration and example to you. Examine whether you're shortchanging your list because there are voices around you telling you that you can't have what you want.

What Do You Fantasize About?

Now that you are in the mindset of questioning the norms that have been presented to you by friends, family, neighbors, and community, challenge yourself to spend some time thinking about your wildest dreams. As I suggest that, I'm smiling at the contradiction between what I'm asking you to do and what society tell us:

It's nice to have wild dreams, but you really must temper them.

Society seems to thrive on setting low expectations and settling. It's time to remove the bridle from your wild dreams and experiment with writing them down. Write down the craziest ones you can imagine. Just because you write them down, doesn't mean that you have to pursue them. The exercise alone is extremely freeing and fun. You may even come across a dream that you decide is worthy of migrating to the list of what you're going to create for yourself.

Do You See Any Patterns?

Here is another story of a client who came to me because she was feeling unfulfilled in her current career. She had also recently divorced and desired more financial independence than she had in the past.

As we talked over the course of many months, it became clear to her that she had never been comfortable dealing with money or the role that money plays in her security and ability to live a comfortable life. The fear-based patterns around money that she had lived with all of her life had kept her stuck in other areas.

She realized that in her fifteen-year marriage, she had always deferred to her wife on financial decisions. She had always told herself that she *wasn't good with money* and that she would always *make just enough to live on* in her line of work. Furthermore, when she really thought about it, she believed that she wouldn't be responsible with the increased income even if she had it.

Someone, way back when, had told her that she was irresponsible with money, and she was shocked to realize that she had chosen to believe that statement. Now that she was living on her own again, she felt free to question these assumptions. Once she did, she became aware of a new job opportunity that was practically staring her in the face. It had the potential to pay her substantially more than she had been making and was still in her line of work.

Yes, she had doubts as we worked through the application process and the salary and benefits negotiation, but she held firm and broke her pattern of believing that she couldn't make a better living and know how to use the increased income responsibly. By the way, she got the job, and immediately had her new employer send a good portion of each paycheck to her retirement savings account.

This story presents an invitation to be aware of patterns. Sometimes patterns are clues to other areas of your life that may need more attention in order to move the rest of your life forward.

Do you see any patterns in what you've written down so far?

Could patterns be preventing you from adding certain dreams to your list?

This book is designed to peel back the layers that may have grown over the goals of your younger self. The time for tempering your expectations is past. Know that you won't break if you don't reach your goals, but you may be extremely disappointed and regretful if you never try.

THIS IS YOU AUTHORING YOUR FUTURE

You know that this book is about creating what you want for yourself. I hope that by now, you are beginning to feel a sense of complete agency, a sense of complete control over the actions you take toward your created future. This is not to be confused with control over everything that happens to you, but rather is meant to heighten your sense of choice in this world. You can spend your life reacting to everything around you or you can spend it creating actions for yourself. The choice is yours.

Is It Ideal?

Go back to your evolving list of what your future looks like. Read it again. Edit it again if you like. Ask yourself the question:

Is it ideal?

Remember that you have permission to remove anything from your list or change anything on your list that is not a *yes* in order to make the list ideal for you.

Let's say you have written down that you are going to change your career slightly so that you work fewer than fifty hours a week. The reason you want to work fewer hours is because you want to have more time to play soccer with your friends, something you're passionate about. Ask yourself:

Is it ideal?

Repeat this question for every item on your list.

There you may pause for a moment and think: *Oh well, it's pretty good.*

The question is:

Is it ideal?

If less than fifty hours a week is not ideal, what is?

Is it forty-five hours or less?

Or, is it between forty and fifty hours, or, something else?

I know this sounds like a ridiculous level of detail.

Let me illustrate with an example what happens when you aren't specific and don't choose measurable ideals. Consider a woman I shall call Marisa, who is actually a compilation of many women I have coached. Marisa was working on her list of what she wanted for herself and wrote down wanting to work Monday to Thursday rather than Monday to Friday. She wanted to take a long hike with her dog and a half day of personal time so that she could garner energy to be present with her kids and accomplish all of the household chores that are required during the weekend.

When Marisa had her annual review at work, she decided to bring this topic up to her supervisor. She got a less-than-stellar reception to the idea. At that point, she threw in the towel and decided that working Monday through Thursday wasn't *in the cards* for her. She proceeded to tell me about all the reasons that continuing on with a Monday-Friday schedule was just fine. She didn't want to discuss the option of creating a way to reach her specific goal. She couldn't see the possibility.

Months later, she was willing to revisit this goal. This time, she stretched her imagination and started applying to similar jobs with different employers in order to expand her pool of possibilities. Two months later, she had landed two interviews with competing companies and got to the final stage with each where they offered her a position. At each, she asked for the Monday-Thursday schedule with pay being at the same rate she had been making. Both companies agreed.

When she went back to her current employer to tell them she had two job offers and was planning to take one of them, her supervisor listened. The supervisor asked if there was anything they could do to make her stay. She replied that a Monday-Thursday schedule and a $5,000.00 bonus would tip her into choosing to stay. Her wishes were granted. She had been specific, had chosen a measurable outcome, and had been creative about how to achieve that goal.

Remember to be specific and quantify whenever possible. You might replace *less than fifty hours a week* with the number that is actually ideal. What you're aiming for here is not just *good enough*. You're aiming for creating exactly what you want.

Does It Feel Right?

Some people listen to their gut, instinct, inner knowing, or whatever you want to call the small voice inside. Some people are better at listening to their inner voice than others. It doesn't matter how good you think you are at it, start by trusting yourself.

Go through everything you've written on your list for your ideal, created future and ask this question:

Does it feel right?

The question *does it feel right?* is slightly different than the question *is it ideal?*

The meaning of this question slightly differs from the meaning of *is it ideal?*

It examines your physical feelings rather than your mental perceptions. The process remains the same.

You'll want to trust your immediate gut response. This is not a time to over-think your response.

As you look at the first line on your list of things that are going to be a part of your created future, does it feel right: *yes* or *no*?

If it doesn't feel right, indicate that by crossing it out or putting a check mark next to it. There's something about that particular item that's not quite right, and you'll want to go back to that line-item and edit it until it feels right to you.

Is That Everything?

I often travel to downtown San Diego from a close-in suburb to meet my clients. When I make this trek, I use the trolley line, which is San Diego's light-rail transportation line. During the journey, the trolley travels through the middle of a cemetery. Every time the train takes me there, I am reminded that we are here for this life and that it passes by quite quickly. Even if you believe in multiple lives, I hope that you also believe that this one counts.

Imagine that you are in a graveyard. You focus on the fact that this life ends and no one knows exactly how much time they have. With that intense focus, ask yourself:

Is that all?

Have you noted everything you really want to pursue?

If you haven't, now is the time to do it.

Chapter 2

Why Do You Want It?

HOW DO YOU FEEL ABOUT IT?

This section considers feelings. Often people who tend to be more logic-based about planning their life goals will forget to check in with how goals make them feel.

Do your goals make you happy?

The next step in the un-settling process is to inventory how you feel about what you've decided you want in your future life. Consciously ask yourself if your feelings tell you anything about how the goal should be adjusted. Compare how you feel about the life you intend to create with the feelings you are experiencing now, prior to making any changes.

List Your Feelings

Download the worksheets for this section. They can be found at www.lysella.com. Simply list the emotions that you feel about the goals you listed at the beginning of the un-settling process. You'll want to list all of the feelings that emerge.

Your feelings may seem to be positive or negative, but try not to judge them. Allow them to flow. Often, happy feelings like *joy* and *freedom* will also bring up an opposite response such as *scary*. It's not unusual for fear to accompany ideas of pursuing new directions. Don't be concerned if this happens to you. Although I was committed to un-settling, one of the feelings that showed up for me as I did this process was *scared shitless*.

How's that for creative vocabulary?

Check for Physical Manifestation of Feelings

Checking for physical manifestations of your feelings is a way to double-check whether or not the life plan you're designing is true for you. What you first write down or think may not be your full story. Sometimes what comes out first is the socially acceptable answer. It's important to check in with yourself through this process to observe your feelings and make adjustments to your plan if necessary.

Lie down or sit in a comfortable position and close your eyes if you wish. As you think about your list, start at the top of your head and run a scan of your body. Notice if you have any physical responses to the items on your list.

- Do you feel butterflies in your stomach?
- Do your shoulders feel tense or tight?
- Is your breathing slower or faster than normal?

This is a cataloging exercise. Write down all the physical responses you observe.

Think of yourself as a scientist looking at your body objectively, and lovingly asking yourself:

When I think about the future that I'm creating for myself, and I notice the feelings associated with my future, is there a physical response within my body?

All you have to do in this step is observe and note your observations.

Does It Seem Too Good to Be True?

This is the point in the un-settling process where many people have an immediate reaction to what they've just written down on their paper. You've taken the time to envision exactly what you want in detail, and you've cataloged the emotions that you feel about your vision. This is the moment in the process where almost 100 percent of the time, someone says:

- *Well, I can't possibly have this.*
- *This has got to be too good to be true.*
- *This is a pipe-dream.*
- *This isn't reality.*

I mention this now so that you can chuckle a bit at yourself if that's happening to you. Simply observe whether or not this is happening.

If you notice objections coming up and find yourself questioning the process, I challenge you to keep reading and completing the exercises all the way through to the end of the book. Then decide if the un-settling approach is right for you.

WHAT WOULD UN-SETTLING DO?

Reflect on what this new reality that you'll create for yourself is going to accomplish, not only for you, but also for your family and for the world.

Can you see the connection between what you want for yourself and the effect achieving it will have on other areas of your life and your world?

Seeing this connection is an important part of the un-settling process. Many people I have worked with, especially women, feel that wanting something and going after what they want is somehow inherently greedy. If this doesn't apply to you, then you may want to just skim this section. If feelings of greed or guilt apply to you, be sure to complete the exercises so that you can uncover the truth. Going after what you really want usually not only benefits you, but also benefits everybody around you.

What Would It Do For You?

This section is about listing everything that un-settling would do for you. Scan through all the different parts of your life and think about how un-settling would make your life better. Depending on what your goal is, you may come up with small benefits, or you may come up with major benefits. Examples of un-settling benefits are:

- *I'd have more money and would be able to buy a car that's reliable.*
- *I would have more time in my life and would be able to be home for dinner every evening, which is really important to me.*
- *I wouldn't feel anxious all the time.*

It doesn't matter how big or small the benefits are. The point here is to list them out so that you're aware of the ripple effects of this goal on other areas of your life.

What Would It Do for Your Family?

Ask yourself how the future you're creating would affect your family, however you might define your family.

Here's a story of un-settling about my client whom I will call Danielle. Danielle suffered from post-traumatic stress disorder (PTSD) and was concerned about how dealing with her illness would affect her family. She knew what she wanted. Danielle wanted the ability to enjoy everything in her life. She was blessed with a beautiful loving wife, a great kid, and a fabulous job. Danielle could see that her unhappiness and depression were weighing her family down. Even in the depths of PTSD-induced depression, she could see taking action would help both her and her family live happier lives.

Danielle bravely committed to un-settling. She sought treatment for her PTSD and found therapy and medications that relieved most of her symptoms. As she went through this process, she saw a gradual improvement in her ability to do her work well and noticed a reduction in the number of fights she had with her wife. Her child also seemed more content. Danielle's initial resistance to getting treatment had been replaced with a feeling of gratitude for having pushed herself to explore treatment options.

A year or so after our first meeting, we were sitting together, having a glass of wine, and reflecting on how joyful she is now.

She said to me, "Yeah, every once in a while I'm tempted to be the victim, but being the victim doesn't pay the bills."

She said it with a chuckle, a smile, and a pure sense of joy. It was apparent what un-settling had done for Danielle and her family.

What Would It Do for the World?

Stopping long enough to think about what un-settling yourself will do for the world is one of the most powerful and exciting parts of the process. When you were young, you may have had dreams of making a global impact, affecting people on a large scale, or bettering the world in some notable way. As adults, most people believe that what they do in their daily lives doesn't have a far-reaching impact.

It's easy to think that what you do doesn't matter when it, in fact, does. Force yourself to think about how what you choose to do with your life every day matters to the world. It matters to your happiness and the people you with whom you interact. Your daily choices regarding what to do with yourself, how to spend your time, and your plans for the future have an impact on the world in some way. Take the time and ask yourself what effect creating your un-settled future will have on the world. Pull out all the stops and recognize your impact. Note your responses on the appropriate worksheet.

IS THERE ANY PART OF YOUR *WHY* THAT MAKES YOU UNCOMFORTABLE?

Why does society dub certain desires and actions as right or wrong?

Here you will consider the idea of social norms and learn why they exist. You will be asked to identify which of the norms you currently adhere to, and whether there are norms or beliefs that you may want to change.

Social Norms and Why They Exist

Let's review a quick history of social norms. This is not meant to be a sociology dissertation, but a simple explanation of why social norms exist. I believe that social norms exist because they define a culture. People are raised within one or more cultures. There are rules of engagement that make societies function. Social norms vary from the mundane activities such as whether you eat with a knife and fork, or with chopsticks, to much larger over-arching social norms, or rules, such as when it's acceptable to kill another person.

Every religion and every law system has rules about acceptable and unacceptable behavior. Rules exist to keep social order. As children, people are taught the social norms of their cultures by well-meaning parents and other people of influence so they will know how to function and survive within the system.

Do You Adhere to Any Social Norms That You've Never Questioned?

Social norms serve a purpose. You are taught these norms by your parents and by others, usually out of a desire to protect you and equip you to operate well in the world. Once you are an adult, you are free to decide whether you want to reprogram yourself regarding any of the social norms that may or may not serve you any longer.

For example, social norms around money are especially sensitive. Some cultures, individuals, and families have negative beliefs about the acquisition of money, whether explicitly stated or simply passed down through connotation and conversations. Some believe that money is evil or sinful, and that wanting it is bad. If that happens to be a part of your story and social norm, and it gets in the way of your earning potential, examine whether you want to make up a new social norm for yourself going forward.

It's a Matter of Perspective

Social norms vary by family, culture, social sub-group, and country. Therefore, it's useful to think about your perspective regarding the social norms that impact you. If you have decided to question and possibly adopt a new social norm around something in your life that is not serving you well, know that you are not alone. Probably some other group, tribe, culture, family, or friend already practices your rewritten social norm.

To illustrate this idea, consider the acquisition of wealth. Your social norm says that any acquisition of wealth above and beyond what it takes to cover your basic needs of shelter, food and clothing is greedy. If you choose to challenge this belief, you may choose to adopt a new social norm that says that the acquisition of wealth means that you are performing at your best in this world. You use your skills at the top of your game. People exchange money for use of your skills. Money that you earn as an exchange allows you to accomplish good in the world. You give to charities that you admire. You treat friends to experiences that they'll remember for a long time. You no longer view the acquisition of wealth as greedy.

If you've decided to change your perspective about a norm, but you find that you don't have the social support around you to sustain that change, it's often good to look elsewhere. Find others who already live the social norm that you want to live. You'll see from associating with them that your change of perspective will serve you better going forward.

The subject of social norms is exciting to explore. The more you question your social norms and doubt their absolute truth in your life today, the more completely you can contribute to the world. You may discover other realities you will claim as your own.

I encourage you to be an explorer. Recognize that the fun of humanity is seeing the different variations and social systems that explain our existence. The joy of being alive in today's day and age is that we can choose what serves us best. So go explore. Discover other perspectives and then choose. And, maybe, the tide of women choosing the norms that benefit them and don't hold them back will one day create a world where women from every part of society throughout the world can live to their fullest potential.

Chapter **3**

What's Stopping You?

MAKE A LIST

Listing on paper both the conscious and unconscious reasons why you've settled helps you evaluate the truth of your statements. The reason for listing it all is to dump anything that may be cluttering your mind and getting in the way of your reaching your goals. It replaces confusion with clarity.

Who Is Stopping You?

Blame is the easiest excuse people reach for when something gets in the way of achieving their goals. Everyone does it, even though it's rarely productive.

Who is preventing you from being who you want to be, getting what you want to get, and doing what you want to do?

Think about the people you are blaming or assigning responsibility to for your life outcomes. Write down the names of those people. This is a necessary step in the un-settling process and will be the beginning of listing the things, people, and circumstances that you believe are stopping you from creating the life that you want to create for yourself.

What Circumstances Are Stopping You?

Remember my friend, Cosette, whom I mentioned earlier in the book?

She is someone who, at times in her life, thought that she might let circumstances stop her. Her situational circumstance was poverty. She chose not to let poverty stop her. Cosette didn't use her poverty as an excuse. I share her story to encourage and inspire you in your own circumstances.

Sometimes your circumstance is that you have to pick up your kid at four o'clock from daycare. Sometimes your circumstance is privilege that raises others' expectations of you too high. You may feel silly writing down your circumstance as an excuse for not getting what you want.

Consider the wealthy woman who felt that her social status prevented her from being a beginning-level dancer in an on-stage recital because she wondered: *What will people think?*

Another professional, middle-class woman believed that she couldn't ask for something different because, she told herself: *Compared to most of my co-workers, I have it really good.*

List the circumstances in your life that prevent you for going after what you want. Nobody's judging you. Nobody else is looking at this list.

Be truthful with yourself about what goes through your head when you ask yourself:

What's keeping me from doing this or from getting that?

As you add your circumstances to the list, don't question their validity. Write down any circumstances that occur to you.

Anything Else?

This is your chance to explore anything and everything that comes to mind when you question yourself about what's stopping you. It could be lack of education, lack of certain skills, or lack of knowledge about how to do X, Y, or Z. Any thoughts that come to mind as reasons why you haven't been able to un-settle yourself should be added to your list now. Double check your mind to make sure you have added every possible obstacle that stands in the way of reaching your goal.

THEY'RE ALL EXCUSES

Sometimes this statement will raise the hair on the back of people's necks and make them defensive — *the whole point is to get your attention, either positive or negative.*

If you examine everything that you've put on your list of reasons, circumstances, or people stopping you from reaching your goal, you will find that you can convert each of your statements into a creative solution.

That's why they're all excuses, and only excuses. If you look around, you'll find countless stories of people who have been given the worst circumstances and have figured out a way to accomplish their goals regardless of their circumstances. No, the playing field is not level — not even close! But no one has a monopoly on grit and determination. You are capable of rising above your circumstances and un-settling.

Let's Be Blunt

This section of the book is not aimed at stroking your ego nor leading you into a space that allows you to continue to feel bad for yourself.

I don't know if I can properly convey a sense of empathy as well as a sense of urgency through writing. If I were standing beside you, I would hope to convey both in my body language, facial expressions, and the way

I listen to you. Being blunt is not about attacking or critiquing you or how you think. The reasons that are keeping you from un-settling are real for you.

I'm being, as some of my clients call me, a loving drill sergeant. I love you, and I understand why we all come up with excuses. I do it, too. Even when you have excuses, being blunt is meant to open your eyes to the fact that you have the possibility to choose to do something different.

You Have Choices

The images and stories that come to mind for me in connection with choices are the images of prisoners of war, holocaust survivors, or other visions of people placed in horrific, inhumane situations. Reading the stories of the people who have come out of those situations alive, with a sense of goodness and belief in the goodness of humanity, are amazing. Through inconceivable hardship, those survivors realized that they were absolutely in control of their perception of the world and of their thoughts. They chose to focus on hope and love.

This is a powerful reminder that you have choices, even when it doesn't feel like you have choices.

If people placed in the most horrid of human conditions can retain the freedom of choice, you can, too. If people stripped of every liberty can still choose feelings of love over hate, so can you. They could have made the mental choice to hate humanity, but they didn't. Their stories are the ultimate illustration of freedom of choice. Thinking of choice this way can help you to keep your own choices in perspective. Remembering these examples might knock some sense into you when you're having a pity party.

Is it easier now to examine your own situations and to see that you always have a choice?

Growing Up — Taking Full Responsibility Isn't Easy

It's so easy to blame your partner, your parents, or your ex who bullied you when you're unhappy about your life. I am extremely guilty of the blaming-my-partner scenario and spent quite a few years of my marriage blaming my husband for my unhappiness. He would've been on my list of people who were stopping me from getting what I wanted.

I would have framed it in statements of blame such as:

He doesn't contribute enough around the house, doesn't say the right things, doesn't do the right things, and therefore, I am unhappy.

My coach made a magical statement to me when I was complaining about all the things that my husband did that kept me from getting what I wanted.

She said, "I think you married exactly who you needed to marry."

She gracefully pointed out to me that I knew exactly who I was getting when I married my husband. She was able to get me to refresh my memory and then to move on. I was reminded that my husband is not responsible for my happiness. I am the only person responsible for my happiness. I was also reminded that it was also my choice to be married every day.

If I was unwilling to grow up and take control of my own happiness, there was no way I could possibly teach other people to do the same. I chose to take responsibility and to define being married as a daily choice that I make. When I approach marriage in this fashion, it feels less like a blame game and more like a choice of partnership that I am making for that day. This daily choice brings my focus into the moment so that I can create the agreement that I'd like to have that day. It also keeps me from dwelling on what happened yesterday or five years ago.

DID I MENTION THAT THEY'RE ALL EXCUSES?

You may be thinking:

Why is this woman going on about excuses?

The entire last section dealt with excuses.

Did she forget to edit this?

The answer is *no*, I didn't forget to edit this, and *yes* there is more to share about excuses because this is the hardest part for us to learn. When you start to take full responsibility for your choices and stop blaming other people for your outcomes and circumstances, you achieve a high that is unlike any other. It's fun. It's joyful to live in a place of adulthood, recognizing your ability to choose.

Think about excuses, discuss the topic with other people, and press yourself to grow beyond them. You may find yourself laughing with me and many others who are traveling down the same path.

But, He Didn't Empty the Dishwasher

Now, I share a story about my own personal dilemma involving the division of household chores.

My husband and I have an agreement that he empties the dishwasher and I load it. The agreement was made with our personal preferences in mind. I hate the noise of clinking when you take the dishes out of the dishwasher, and he doesn't like to fiddle with placing oddly-shaped items in a dishwasher, which I enjoy.

Occasionally my husband doesn't empty the dishwasher. When that happens, it's easy for me to take that one simple act and turn it into something bigger in my mind than not emptying the dishwasher.

I can make it mean:

- *He doesn't love me.*
- *He doesn't respect me.*
- *He doesn't respect our division of labor.*
- *He doesn't honor our agreement.*
- *I thought I married a feminist, but he isn't acting like a feminist.*
- *Our marriage is falling apart.*
- *I have to do everything around here.*

I know with certainty that I can't know what my husband's intentions are unless I ask him. I know now that when my husband doesn't empty the dishwasher he simply doesn't empty the dishwasher.

You get the picture. Don't let your mind run away with its made-up stories about what other people's actions mean.

Using Agreements to Banish Excuses

This concept comes from the coach, Steve Chandler, and it might well save your business and personal life. Steve professes that most people carry around expectations without making agreements, setting themselves up for disappointment and unhappiness and, ultimately, allowing us to blame others in order to have an excuse. Setting clear agreements is his proposed solution for banishing excuses from your life. He proposes we switch from having expectations to asking for agreements. This allows for clear communication. It also gives a framework for improvement. If an agreement stumbles upon a grey area, your task simply becomes to make a better agreement. In the land of expectations, grey areas create excuses and blame. This is a powerful concept.

Here's a classic example of Steve's theory. Let's say that you have an employee who you're starting to think is irresponsible or a low performer. You're at the point where you are asking yourself why you are plagued with irresponsible employees. You ask yourself why you can't find dedicated people anymore.

In my book, that way of thinking lands squarely in the excuse category. If you believe there is at least some truth to be had in the idea that you can choose to make your employees great, then read on for an example. This is a story about how to convert your expectations—which lead to you making up excuses for not having stellar employees—into agreements where the definition of stellar is explicitly measurable and agreed upon.

Suppose on Friday you ask your employee to complete a certain project, and she says she will do it. By Tuesday, you find yourself champing at the bit, wondering where the completed project is.

You start to build up resentment and think: *Ugh, she's not a very good employee, she turns things in late.*

When your employee finally gives you the project on Thursday, you're already worked up and you say, "Well, why are you giving this to me now? I expected it to be done on Tuesday."

You *expected* the work to be done on Tuesday, but you didn't share your expectation with your employee. You didn't say anything about the due date.

Have you ever found yourself in this kind of situation?

You could have avoided frustration and resentment had you taken the time to complete the circle with your employee.

First, you could have said, "Here's a project I'd like you to take on. Are you willing to do it?"

That's asking for agreement. You're getting a *yes* or *no*.

Next, you could ask, "Are you willing and able to complete this project by Tuesday?"

That's indicating your expectation and again asking for agreement. You're getting a *yes* or *no*. Using this method prevents frustration and opens up clear channels of communication.

Making agreements is often called *buy-in*. When you're a party to a bona fide agreement, you and the other parties have participated and negotiated what you and they are willing to do. Everyone gives their word to keep the promises made. Buy-in is powerful and produces results, especially when all expectations are clearly stated.

Using this approach can also un-settle broken relationships at work or in your personal life. Once we realize that all relationships are ongoing projects that require creating and refining agreements over time, we can stop using catch-all character descriptions as excuses for poor relationships.

Rather than an employee or a spouse being *irresponsible* for not meeting your expectations, you have an agreement about a particular task. Either that agreement is kept or it is not. When it's not, you can troubleshoot the agreement rather than the other person's character.

And, of course, if agreements are continually made and then broken, it's obvious to you both that the relationship is probably not meant to be.

It's Just You and the Mirror When There's No One Left to Blame

When you strip away the blame that you might be assigning to circumstances or people for your inability to un-settle yourself, what's left?

Look at yourself in the mirror.

What do you see?

Are you able to see a person:

- Who's ready to take full responsibility and sees the value in doing so?
- Who's ready to make conscious choices that work for you?
- Who knows you're not perfect and that you'll make mistakes?
- Who's ready to start taking the steps that get you closer to what you're up to in this world?

You'll be able to march down this path of freedom and joy, knowing that you get to choose your future.

If I could leave you with one exercise here, it would be to pick something in your life that you still believe you have no control over. Challenge yourself to get creative.

Perhaps you want to go back to school, but you own a home and the mortgage payments strap your budget.

You may think: *Well I can't possibly go back to school because I have a mortgage to pay, and I can't do both at the same time.*

What are your choices?

If you choose to pay a mortgage, you are also choosing not to go to school. You could choose to sell your house and live in a one-bedroom apartment while you go to school. Your choices may not be comfortable, but you do have choices.

Everyone makes choices, none of them are right or wrong. You need to be creative and look at all your options.

Some may seem extreme, but by examining all of the possibilities, you can no longer believe: *I don't have a choice.*

You always have a choice. It's a matter of deciding whether that trade-off is worth it to you.

Chapter 4

Are You Ashamed or Scared? — The Crying Chapter

WHAT HAVEN'T YOU WRITTEN DOWN YET THAT YOU KNOW IS STILL CASTING A SHADOW OVER THIS PROCESS?

When I'm sitting face to face with someone, this is the time in the discovery process when I can tell by their body language if they're holding something back. There may be more that they are yearning to add to the list of what they have settled for and want to un-settle. However, to this point they have not been willing to write it down or tell me about it.

If you were with me in person, I would ask you if there is anything else. Then I'd be silent. I'd let us sit in uncomfortable silence while you dig all the way down to your deepest desires. I'd encourage you to bring up the goals that seem ridiculously out of reach. To reach for the dreams you may even be ashamed to ask for. I cannot think of an instance in which clients couldn't discover one more item to explore.

What Haven't You Told Me?

As I mentioned in the introduction, this book allows me to share the un-settling process with more women than I could possibly meet in person. My mission is to help you find the courage to un-settle and act now to create the life you love.

Imagine I'm in front of you. If you haven't ever met me in person, or you haven't seen me, you can go to my website at www.lysella.com or my Facebook page at "Un-settling by Lys Ella Severtson" to get a sense of who I am. You can see a video of me if you want to see how I look and what my voice is like.

As you see me looking into the camera's eye, pretend that I'm sitting across the table from you. I'm speaking to you.

Pretend that I'm asking you: *What haven't you told me?*

I ask it with sincerity. I ask it with kindness and love, and, also with a bit of pressure. I'm asking you — whether spoken or unspoken:

What haven't you told me?

What is a little bit scary?

What do you not want me to know?

The stuff that your real dreams are made of is the stuff that feels a little scary and that you're reluctant to share. Your rational mind plays just below the surface and gets in the way of your digging deeper to uncover what you really want. Be aware that your rational mind will edit for you and convince you that you can't have what you want.

This is a recurring story among my clients. The client is usually a professional woman, in her mid-thirties, with one or two young children. She comes to me wanting to figure out how the heck to achieve this thing called *work-life balance*.

Repeatedly, I ask, *What else do you want?*

Suddenly, the design she's creating for herself takes a turn, and she tells me what she really wants.

She tells me about the flexibility that she wants to have in her life. She tells that flexibility, to her, does not mean that she's still working fifty hours a week in an office and can leave every once in a while at three o'clock to pick up her kids from school. That's not what she wants. What she really wants is something drastically different.

She wants to work twenty to thirty hours a week. She wants to be trusted to do great thinking outside of those hours, and she wants to be paid accordingly. She wants to have time to stay fit and go to the gym or run with her friends. That's what she really wants, and she wants to still make the salary that she makes right now. That's the part she wasn't willing to tell me, until I asked the question.

Unworthiness, Shame, and Guilt

Unworthiness, shame, and guilt are lumped into the same category, because they all have self-imposed definitions that can hinder your creative thought process. Thoughts of unworthiness, shame, and guilt can get in the way of imagining and writing down your dream or goal, the first step in creating what you want.

In the client scenario about the mid-thirties woman, these three feelings were the reasons she was afraid to share what she wanted at the beginning of the conversation.

Usually her answer is something like, "I don't deserve that," or, "It would be shameful if I were to get that and others didn't."

Any self-imposed judgment about what your future *should* look like is something I'd encourage you to consider reclassifying.

Remember our discussion about social norms?

Just because somebody told you when you were little what was acceptable behavior for women, or because what you see around you is different from what you want, doesn't make what you want a shameful thing. *Why* you believe what you currently believe is not important. What is important is to be aware of these judgments if they come up for you. They are only stories that you've made up about unworthiness, shame, and guilt. You have the choice to create new stories.

This Isn't Therapy, But It's Okay to Cry

Disclaimer: This section may bring tears. Usually when I'm meeting with people one-on-one, we're in a private situation, so it doesn't matter if somebody tears up, or cries it all out. I'm okay with it, and they trust me enough to be okay with it, too. Since I don't know where you are when you're reading this, I've given you the warning up-front. If you don't like to cry in public, or in the company of others, you might want to save this section for a time when you're in private.

The reason you may cry is because you will be digging deeper into why you aren't fully asking for what you want. You may associate what you want with guilt, shame, or unworthiness. As you dig deeper, you may have emotional revelations. You might cry. It's okay to cry.

YOU'RE NOT ALONE

Remind yourself that you're not alone. You can exhale a sigh of relief knowing that others have faced the challenges you're up against right now.

These Feelings Are More Common Than You Think

There are clear lines determined by social norms that delineate what's appropriate to share in social situations, intimate relationships, and with your closest friends and family. Most people are very careful about what they share.

Beyond the social norms, there are specific rules of engagement among different families and different relationships around the depth and the breadth of the topics that are shared. It's extremely common for people to avoid talking about the *scary stuff*. The discussion of feelings such as worthiness, guilt, and shame are often viewed as off limits.

If it makes you feel any better or more normal, do this exercise. Look around your office, the coffee shop, or wherever you happen to be at this moment. Know that nine out of ten people you see probably have some version of the same worry, fear, anxiety, or feeling of unworthiness that you experience right now. It's there, it's real, and it's unspoken. Consider yourself to be one step ahead because you're actually *doing* something about it.

These Feelings Have a Societal Function

Feelings of worthiness, shame, and guilt have societal functions. They are three mechanisms that humans use to define their place in the world and understand the difference between right and wrong within our social groups so as to keep order. Because humans are emotional, physical, and social beings, they rely on mechanisms to maintain structure within their social groups. As worthiness, shame, and guilt relate to your feelings about your un-settled future, consider distancing yourself from them if they are giving you any heartburn throughout the exercises.

Unworthiness

Think back to the first time you can remember someone telling you that you didn't deserve something that you wanted or that you already had. To help you, a worksheet for this section is available at www.lysella.com.

Got it in your mind?

What was it?

Worthiness can be defined as your permission to exist in this world in your particular body.

My earliest memory of worthiness was not an explicit statement, but rather a set of beliefs and behaviors held by my grandparents who passed it along to me. Their set of beliefs and behaviors clearly communicated their definition of a virtuous and therefore worthy person. A worthy person was one who not only cared immensely about being kind to others, but who also actively attempted to own very few worldly possessions and tried to always be materially humble.

I didn't remember this until well into adulthood when I was struggling with the notion of creating a business that might create wealth rather than simply creating a subsistence income.

My immediate internal thoughts were:

Who are you to deserve wealth?

You're not worthy.

After some consideration, I came to the conclusion that everyone is worthy. Once I applied this kinder definition of worthiness to myself, I was able to move on with un-settling my life and getting on board with my plan to create the life I wanted to create.

You are worthy, too.

Shame

Shame can be a powerful emotion. It's a punishment mechanism that humans have used since the dawn of time to discourage certain behavior. For example, if a culture does not want people killing each other, there can be many ways to punish that. One could be a physical consequence like banishing them from your community or physically punishing them in return.

There are other ways of putting people in their place, like shaming. Shame is a strong emotional tactic, one that is understood by all humans. Think of the pillory in the public square. A pillory is a device formerly used for publicly punishing offenders. A constructed wooden frame with holes in it held and locked the head and hands. The pillory exposed offenders to public scorn or ridicule. It was deliberately placed in public to inform onlookers of unacceptable behavior.

Is there something on your list that you consider to be shameful?

Is it something that the culture you were raised in considers to be shameful?

Did you associate shame with that thing on your list at some other point in your life even if you no longer consider it to be shameful?

Regardless of where the label came from, note it now. You can decide if you want to remove the label later.

Guilt

When you feel guilty, it's because you have done something that you believe was wrong even if the action was hidden or secret. Once a society has rules for what is right and wrong, guilt becomes a handy self-imposed reinforcement.

If a group decides that an action, such as women going on unescorted dates, is wrong, the group will employ shame to call out the transgressors. Because shaming is often public, everyone in the social group understands that the action is a no-no. Shaming educates the youngest members of the group as to what is unacceptable. Once understood, then those newest members of the group will self-impose guilt if they do something that was on the unacceptable list.

So, guilt serves as the self-imposed mechanism to maintain a social norm. Therefore, if you perform the action, but do not get *caught*, you will most likely feel guilt.

What's on your guilt list?

Just write it down. No one is looking.

These norms and emotions exist in order to keep people's behavior in check. Understanding the functions of these labels on a societal level frees you to consider how the norms affect you on a personal level. You can choose what you label as shame, guilt, and worthiness in your own life.

Learn to Question

Learning to question is probably one of the most powerful habits you can gain as an adolescent and adult. Children are born curious. They ask *why* all the time to figure out their social system and how to live in it. As they construct their lives, they ask *why* so that they know the rules of the game.

You grow into adulthood with a good understanding of the rules of the game. Your understanding is filtered by where you grew up, how you grew up, who your parents are, and who your friends were. You can train yourself as an adult to re-learn the skill of questioning:

- What is worthy?
- Why do you do the things you do?
- What labels do you assign to feelings and actions?

Answer these questions and you will continue to learn and grow.

Questioning is a child-like activity that can bring more joy into your life. It allows you to see life with wonder and approach your choices with excitement, from a child's point of view. Children see life as limitless.

DO YOU WANT TO BELIEVE A NEW STORY?

This is one of the most fun sections of this book; you get to choose to do something differently than you've done it in the past.

Do you want to choose a new system or pattern in order to create different results?

The following exercises will explore whether you are ready to believe and create a new story for yourself. If you are, there are instructions to guide you.

Is the Unworthiness, Shame, or Guilt Useful to You?

Is it useful?

The question is deceptively simple.

Asking yourself this question can be a powerful and freeing tool. While there is a societal function for each of these feelings, people often over-apply them to their daily lives in ways that don't help them or the society around them. Let's look at guilt, for example.

In the process of developing her strategy for un-settling herself, one client recognized that she felt guilt about having moved far away from her parents. When asked if feeling guilty was useful to her, she said it wasn't. I asked her why it wasn't useful.

She said, "Well, because, I can be guilty, and punish myself for having made that choice, but it doesn't put me back in my hometown near my parents, which is the part that I feel most guilty about. Feeling guilty also takes up space in my mind and in my heart that I could better use doing things that will create a nicer life for myself, and even a nicer life for my parents."

Do you see the value in questioning yourself about the usefulness of unworthiness, shame, or guilt in your life?

What Would Your New Story Be?

Sharpen your pencil because this is your time to craft a new story.

What will you create?

Think about my client's issues with guilt as an example to guide you.

If you were this woman and felt guilt for having left the city where your parents live, what would your new story about that choice be?

Her new story might be something like this:

> *I chose to leave the city where my parents live because I was lured by the opportunities and the excitement that come along with living in a larger city. All of those opportunities are giving me a life that I never could have experienced back home. I treasure these new experiences. I realize that the choice to move has made me a better, happier, and more complete person. When I feel happier, I am also a better daughter to my parents.*

What could your new story be?

If you'd like, write a few versions of your story so that you can test them out to see which feels most authentic to you.

Try It On for a Week

This is a fun exercise and can often be a way to test out a new story, especially if it feels uncomfortable to you. Some women have a hard time creating a new story for themselves. Even though your current story may have been written long ago and may not work for you today, it is familiar and comfortable. To un-settle yourself and create a new story, you need to remind yourself that old and familiar doesn't mean permanent.

Have you ever traveled alone to a foreign country where you don't speak the language?

Writing your new story can feel like being in a place where no one knows you or your story. You can try on whatever story you want. You can be whoever you want to be. As you craft your new story, think of yourself as an adventurer in a foreign land. See how it feels to try on and adjust your story to fit you.

If writing your story feels challenging, ask yourself how your best friend would tell your new story. Try your new story on for a week or even a day and see if it feels right to you.

Chapter 5

What Are You Willing to Do About It?

ACTIONS ARE ALL THAT MATTER

Taking action moves you from a state of dreaming about something that you want to create to actually un-settling yourself to do it. This is where the rubber hits the road!

The hard part of any change is taking actions even when you don't feel like it and don't know what to do next. Even if you don't think you're ready, don't worry. You can count on me to be there with you to listen and guide you. Remember that the community of women who are un-settling themselves is ready to welcome you should you need a pep talk. We're on Facebook at "Un-settling by Lys Ella Severtson."

Doing Versus Learning

We live in an era when any information we could possibly want is available to us. The difference between consuming information in order to learn about something and learning in order to take action is important to understand in the context of un-settling yourself.

A classic example of this difference can be related to the excitement that you feel after you've heard a dynamic public speaker. The speech may have triggered excitement about something you *could do* in your future, but until you *do* something with the information you've learned, it is only information.

There are multiple right ways to take action and sometimes it doesn't matter which of those you choose. Rather than focusing on how to do something, or needing to know the particular system that guarantees you will achieve what you want, just keep going. Use the information that you currently have, continue learning, and take persistent action to move forward.

Don't Wait for Perfect

Perfection is elusive. If you've ever worked on a project or a deliverable and felt as if you had to keep going until it was perfect, you most likely never felt satisfied with your work. The longer you wait for perfection, the higher the probability that you will never make the change, deliver the product, or release the invention.

Iteration is the way to go. According to Merriam-Webster, *iteration* is:

A procedure in which repetition of a sequence of operations yields results successively closer to a desired result.

Let's break it down.

Your procedure is a commitment to taking actions rather than stalling. Taking multiple micro-actions one after the other is your *repetition of a sequence of operations*. Your ultimate goal of un-settling is your *desired result*.

What is your desired result, your procedure, and your sequence of operations that you'll be repeating.

The Facebook page has the worksheets for this exercise.

Iteration is a faster learning and growing process to use than attempting your entire un-settling plan at once. It allows you to quickly test small changes and receive real-world feedback. You can add to the system as you begin to see favorable results, fixing what needs to be fixed as you go along, instead of spending all your time on extensive planning. Start to get feedback and get real-time learning rather than continuing to operate in your own head.

Test It

Remember how you tried on your new story in the last chapter?

The process for taking actions is similar and involves testing out your action steps. Testing out small actions one at a time makes it easier to start your un-settling plan. Small actions reduce feelings of fear and make the process feel more approachable. Testing allows you to ease into your un-settling process before you make a long-term commitment to it.

If something feels scary, remind yourself that you are just testing it out to see if it works for you. It's like a free trial. Experiment to see if you like the new action better than the previous one. You won't know if you like it or not until you try it. After your first test, evaluate your feelings. You'll see where you're on track and where your actions need to be tweaked. Edit as needed and test it again. Use the worksheets from the Facebook page to help you.

THE PSYCHOLOGY OF SETTING MICRO-GOALS

Setting micro-goals is different from the kind of goal-setting that most people are accustomed to. The concept is helpful to use when starting movement toward a goal and maintaining momentum along the way. Micro-goals start with a typical goal that you modify to improve your odds of achieving it.

Creating a Micro-Goal

For this section, pick a goal and write it down. A worksheet is available www.lysella.com.

How would you feel if you knew that you were 100 percent guaranteed to reach your goal by the deadline you have set?

Transforming your goal by breaking it into much smaller pieces, or *micro-goals*, can help you succeed.

Here's an example of how that transformation plays out. I'm working with a writer who defines un-settling herself as writing on a consistent basis. Her goal is to write for an hour each day. In order to transform her goal into a micro-goal, I asked her a series of questions:

- *Is your week Monday through Friday?*
- *Do you intend to write seven days a week?*
- *Tell me about the rest of this week.*
- *Is there anything happening in your life that would prevent you from writing an hour each day?*

She responded, "Oh, yea, well now that I think about it, my daughter has baseball practice on Wednesday, and, oh my parents are coming in from out-of-town Thursday and Friday, so that might be really hard to get the hour done on those days."

This is a perfect example of when a micro-goal is most appropriate. My client decided to downsize her goal to a micro-goal in order to fit her situation. After going through the series of questions again, she decided that she could commit to writing for five minutes each day with 100 percent certainty of follow through. That's a micro-goal.

Make your micro-goal so easy that you are 100 percent guaranteed to win. You can edit any goal using this process and be certain you will reach your goal in the timeline you set.

Why Winning Matters

It's important to win. And, building up a series of wins is important to our psyche. The cool thing about the brain is that it doesn't care how small the win is. For whatever reason — a brain scientist would have to explain — it seems that the brain counts a *small win* just as much as a *big win*.

If you find that to be true for your brain, why not give it more *small wins*?

Using micro-goals allows you to win in your own mind. You may find that you begin a project excited about what you're creating, but then lose your enthusiasm if you run into obstacles. Obstacles often show up because your goals are too large to manage. Using micro-goals, you can break any goal down into achievable steps that allow you to build up your wins. Winning helps you stay motivated throughout the process of reaching your goal.

A micro-goal helps you move psychologically towards your end game. When you set achievable goals and know that you are 100 percent guaranteed to win, you will probably put in extra effort to go a littler farther than you planned. Not only have you completed that goal, but you've demonstrated that you're a winner by reaching farther than you thought possible. Winning builds up your momentum and sets you up to win again.

Repeat

In the process of un-settling, you will set micro-goals repeatedly. Repetition is the key to your success. Any time you find yourself stuck at any step in your plan, revisit the micro-goal concept, and repeat the process.

Let's look back at the writer's example. She stuck to her plan of writing for five minutes each day until something happened, and she *fell off the wagon*. She lost her momentum and felt bad that she hadn't been writing.

Do you think this might be a good time for the writer to repeat the micro-goal process?

She might commit to writing for one minute at night before she goes to bed to get back on track. You have to regroup when you're feeling stuck. Make a tiny goal. Preferably, it should be a goal you can complete that day. If you keep repeating one micro-goal at a minimum each day, you're guaranteed to reach the finish line.

FOCUS ON ONE, NOT MANY

The concept of slowing down and focusing on one goal comes from the coach, Steve Chandler. He advocates focusing intently on one task, problem, or step at a time. Rather than worrying about all the steps you need to take before you cross the finish line, magnify your view of the step immediately in front of you. This approach is useful in the un-settling process because it helps you to clearly focus your mind on the first action in your plan before you move on to the next.

I'm a Human, Not a Sardine

You're going to need help to accomplish what you are setting out to do. That help will involve other humans, some of whom you haven't yet met.

I'm a human, not a sardine sums up the way you can inadvertently make people feel..

We humans require some delicate care that other animals—such as fish—might not need. We like to be treated as individuals. Remember to treat the people who will ask to help you like human beings by paying close, focused attention to each individual with whom you interact.

When your un-settling leads you to ask someone for advice, an introduction, or referral, remember they are not a sardine. Remember to look people in the eyes. Remember to talk slowly, thank people for their help, and to spontaneously reciprocate when you can. Small things like not answering your phone while talking to someone and not leaving the conversation as soon as someone *better* enters the room can go a long way towards demonstrating to the person in front of you that they are important to you.

Humans know the difference between being treated respectfully, and being treated like a dispensable commodity. Be sure to focus on the person whose advice you've solicited. That person might be able to refer you to other people who are willing to help you un-settle. Genuinely and purposefully connect with other people. Mass marketing and social media can never replace the power of a personal, one-to-one connection with another human being.

What is one way you can increase the humanity of your own connections?

Write it down on the worksheet.

Slow Down

The concept of slowing down is a component of focusing on one, and not many. Slowing down can create more focus across all areas of your life. Slow down your conversations. Allow more appointment time than you think you need. You'll be able to be more present and able to focus on the one task or one person in front of you.

Don't let *busy* be the equivalent of *productive*.

It is not productive to be running around like a chicken with your head cut off. People often wear that excuse as a badge of honor in today's world by equating busy with important. You've heard people complain about not having enough time to do the things they want to do. Most people make time for what's important to them.

Wouldn't it be nice to exercise?

I'm a working mom, and I don't have the time.

Remember those micro-actions?

Take a moment to write down the most important things to you on the worksheet. Then, guess how much time you have spent in the past seven days doing those things. If there's a mismatch, take a micro-action to start an avalanche of change.

If you wanted to get more exercise, you might start with parking your car a few spaces farther away from the building.

You will find that the most successful people are intensely focused, and know exactly where they spend their time. They recognize that they can't and don't want to do everything and choose wisely. They know when they need to leave a meeting in order to arrive on time to the next one. They're not frazzled. They know how to say *no* to the things in their lives that are useless filler.

On the worksheet, write down the things you spend most of your time doing that are NOT the things you want to be doing.

What micro-action can you take to reduce time spent in these areas?

Learn how to analyze your life, decide what to say *no* to, and then actually say *no* in order to create space for the un-settled version of your life. Start by putting some buffers in your calendar between your appointments so that you don't run late to appointments. Put a *not available* buffer in your calendar and don't schedule appointments that can interrupt your workflow. Using buffers will help you reduce stress.

Imagine what it would be like if you didn't have to choose between dinner at home or finishing your work?

What Would Be of Service?

This is an un-settling question that again sharpens your focus on *one, not many*. Pause before each action that you take, every conversation that you have, and every text or email that you send, and ask yourself:

- What would truly be of service to the people on the receiving end of my message?

- What would be the best way I could show up in this situation to make it efficient, smooth, and enjoyable?

- Will this action or interaction get me closer to the ideal, un-settled version of my life?

You might decide not to engage in the action or interaction if your answers to the questions reveal the intent to be *what can I get out of this?* Worse, you may discover there is no intention behind the action or communication except filler.

Test it out.

Build this process into your day as a way to maximize your time and energy. See what it does for you. I have found that it has improved my relationships and allowed me to spend more time on the things that are most important. I'll be curious to see what it does for you.

Conclusion

I wrote this how-to guide because I don't want you to be lonely anymore. I want you to know that there are other women like you who know that they want something more than what they currently have. Like you, they recognize that their dream or goal may be so far outside their social norms that pursuing their goal feels lonely. You question your sanity at times along your un-settling journey.

My un-settling experience continues to be exciting. Once I understood that there were people who could help me along the path, I became willing to take action despite my fears, and I knew I had to share the experience with you. I hope this book has allowed you to feel the un-settling process for yourself and to connect with other people who are in a similar situation. That's what I want to leave you with.

I want the women who feel moved to un-settle their lives to have a community of women with whom to interact. I want them to continue to grow and to push for better. Any woman who reads this book and is influenced by the stories, philosophy, and ideas that are stated here is invited to join our community and further the conversation at my page, "Un-settling by Lys Ella Severtson" on Facebook.

Next Steps

If you haven't already, please access your worksheets and join the community at the "Un-settling by Lys Ella Severtson" on Facebook.

About the Author

Lys Ella Severtson was a 36-year-old, married, working mother when she started developing her not-so-great plan for leaving her corporate career to start her own business. Through the rocky two years that followed that decision, she noticed that she was not alone in her experience. There was a familiar angst among many of her female, American clients - a feeling that the years of sacrifice and head-down work required by their relationships, children, careers, and everything else, left them feeling like they had settled for a life that wasn't what they wanted.

Roughly 70% of American working-age women are employed outside the home, and most balance paid work with child-rearing, societal expectations of caregiving, and romantic partner relationships - leaving little room to breathe.

Severtson's observations and stories are told in conjunction with a step-by-step guide for learning to identify the kind of life you really want, why you want it, and how to get it.

www.ingramcontent.com/pod-product-compliance
Lightning Source LLC
Chambersburg PA
CBHW071737090426
42738CB00011B/2514